Arrow

SUMITA CHAKRABORTY

Arrow

POEMS

Alice James Books

FARMINGTON, MAINE

alicejamesbooks.org

10 9 8 7 6 5 4 3 2 1

Alice James Books are published by Alice James Poetry Cooperative, Inc., an affiliate of the University of Maine at Farmington.

Alice James Books
114 Prescott Street
Farmington, ME 04938
www.alicejamesbooks.org

Library of Congress Cataloging-in-Publication Data

Names: Chakraborty, Sumita (Poet), author.
Title: Arrow : poems / Sumita Chakraborty.
Description: Farmington, ME : Alice James Books, [2020]
Identifiers: LCCN 2020012199 (print) | LCCN 2020012200 (ebook) | ISBN 9781948579117 (trade paperback) | ISBN 9781948579674 (epub)
Subjects: LCGFT: Poetry.
Classification: LCC PS3603.H33556 A87 2020 (print) | LCC PS3603.H33556 (ebook) | DDC 811/.6--dc23
LC record available at https://lccn.loc.gov/2020012199
LC ebook record available at https://lccn.loc.gov/2020012200

Alice James Books gratefully acknowledges support from individual donors, private foundations, the University of Maine at Farmington, the National Endowment for the Arts, and the Amazon Literary Partnership.

Cover image: "SATELLITE OF MODERN LOVE," Courtesy of E.V. DAY and Carolina Nitsch Contemporary Art, NYC. Interior images: Pocike / Shutterstock, Yullishi / Shutterstock.

CONTENTS

Notes

ACKNOWLEDGMENTS

Language is a skin: I rub my language against the other. It is as if I had words instead of fingers, or fingers at the tip of my words.

— R O L A N D   B A R T H E S ,   *A Lover's Discourse*

I am deeply thankful to the editors and staffs of the following journals, where these poems first appeared, sometimes under different titles and in earlier forms: *American Poetry Review, At Length, Blackbird, BOAAT, Boston Review, Connotation Press: An Online Artifact's A Poetry Congeries, Glass, The Journal, Memorious, The Offing, Poetry, The Rumpus, Stand* (UK), and *Witness*. Many thanks also to the editors and staffs of *The Best American Poetry 2019, PN Review* (UK), and *New Poetries VII* (UK), in which some of these poems have been reprinted.

I would like to thank the Poetry Foundation; the Department of English at the University of Michigan; the Department of English, the Department of Women's, Gender, and Sexuality Studies, and the Fox Center for Humanistic Inquiry at Emory University; and Wellesley College (which gave me my first glimpse of a life beyond the contours of anything I even had the vocabulary then to fathom). I'm especially grateful for the students, colleagues, friends, advisors, and mentors I had the good fortune to meet in these spaces, some of whom I name here, but many more of which exist than could be contained in these pages.

To the brilliant, kind, generous people at Alice James Books and Carcanet Press—Carey, Alyssa, Emily, and Julia at Alice James; Michael, Jazmine, and Andrew at Carcanet; all of the other editors, copy editors, interns, staff members, designers, readers; every office hedgehog and spider and dust bunny—I'm indebted to your keen eyes, your incredible work, and your faith in me. Thank you for doing the work that you do.

To Dan Chiasson, Frank Bidart, and Lucie Brock-Broido, my earliest poetry teachers, for whom no amount of gratitude will ever suffice.

To A. Van Jordan, Cortney Lamar Charleston, Deboleena Roy, Deborah Elise White, Elizabeth Wilson, Emilia Phillips, Emily Jungmin Yoon, Emily Leithauser, Fatimah Asghar, Gillian White, Heather Hughes, Jericho Brown, Jonathan Farmer, Kaveh Akbar, Laura Otis, Linda Gregerson, Lynne Huffer, Maggie Greaves Ozgur, Melissa Green, Nathan Suhr-Sytsma, Nicole Morris, Nomi Stone, Paige Lewis, Rachel Mennies, Roy Guzmán, Sara Eliza Johnson, Susan Reviere, and Walter Kalaidjian, whose gifts of friendship and support mean everything to me, and whose brilliant minds have taught me all I know. To Mitali Chakraborty and Priya Chakraborty, whose blood and ashes respectively I share.

To Taylor Schey: I love you, and no day, night, dawn, or dusk goes by in which I am not so terribly thankful that you exist and are a part of my life.

WORLD

with this A R R O W

I thee wed.

— F R A N K   B I D A R T

MARIGOLDS

Like oak trees swerving out of the hills
And setting their faces to the wind
Day after day being practically lifted away
They are lashed to the earth
And never let go
Gripping on darkness

— A L I C E   O S W A L D , *Memorial*

When I picture Robert, he is in the Public Garden,
watching setting suns, like the ill-fated king, turn all to gold.
Robert with the swans. Robert under the statue of Washington.

Robert amid the tulips. Without a childhood
home, I made for myself a house of orchids, of sewer grates
with fishes on them, of forsythia and maple trees.

Of this I am sure: when Robert crossed the bridge
between Boston and Cambridge, he saw Poseidon.
In late summer, he could tell that underneath

the sailboats is a god, mighty and to be feared.
In midwinter, he alone knew the ice
could not long contain that god.

In the pipes in his home, he heard the gurgle of illness.
I smell illness in the riotous orchid blooms.

What are midnight trees?
I think that once I knew one such tree,
if it is the kind owls gather on nightly

to fight, barking,
eyes dim with bloodlust and the hiss of feathers.
I built for myself a house of orchids, with a cave underneath,

a cave shaped into an armory
brimming with tarantula hawks, giant sparrow bees,
and admiral butterflies.

In place of stalactites hang treeless,
inextricable roots.
O sacred receptacle of my joys.

The day I first learned the word *argonaut*,
I wrote it in a poem. I searched the seas for one.

I searched the skies. I searched a painting.
In the painting, I found the word *spears*, which I drove slowly
into my father's ribs. He I eulogized and he I resurrected,

reaching again for the spears. I have seen
countless full moons fail. Each of them hollowed,
flooding heartfirst the craw-faced light, the bracken

underneath. Then, the sound of a wounded owl,
a soft, sudden darkness in my throat. O, how this villainy.
In mourning, the owls are replaced by hawks.

From one angle, broad-winged hawks
seem to have two pairs of hollow eyes.
We are looking for you, say the kettles of satellites

to the humans lost, to the plane
disappeared, to what lives thirty miles below

the surface of Enceladus. On this morning in April,
Haixun 01, Ocean Shield, and HMS Echo hear a thump
that sounds like the colors inside an oyster shell.

The frequency of the noise can make a heart
stop. Anxious as seaweed, over the sides of the ships
creep hordes of trembling locators.

The satellites stare with breath hitching in their throats.
Between the wine-colored hull of Ocean Shield and Enceladus
lies eight times the distance between Earth and the sun.

Thirty miles below the surface of that geyser-ridden, tiger-striped
Saturnian moon lies life, report the satellites.
The hawks steel their two pairs of eyes up

toward alien oceans on other planets.
What I am is all that I can carry, wrote Deborah.

What can I carry? All that I caught I left behind,
all that I missed, I carried.
The hawks are not looking

toward alien oceans. I am.
I am looking, too, to alien men and women.
I picture hurtling into them, by turn, to serve my lust.

I picture us bent sideways, impaled,
contorted and screaming. I picture
the different shades of a moan.

The word *bed* fills the four eyes in my mind
with the color gold, gold of the ill-fated king
and the Garden sunset, gold glinting in a decaying tooth,

goldenrod, a haze of pollen, the dragon's treasure,
a long necklace of many fine gold chains

reaching down to a woman's hips.
Young woman walks down to the river,
down to the river of gold.

Young woman walks down to the river,
down to the river and drowns.
In the word *bed* also joyously wail

bed the color of ashen near death, *bed* the fleshly color
of bodies broken for good, *bed* the color blue
of heart-stopped lips. O, here I lift this one hand

up to heaven. The ghosts of the poisoned dogs
live in the piano. The ghost of my mother, still living,
lives in her excised tumor and staghorn kidney stone.

The ghost of my ability to love without grief, still living,
lives in this poem. All my pockets filled with stones

in the river I'll be found. Why, then, I am the devil's dam—
dangle me from a cliff, twelve thousand feet above sea.
O, speak with possibilities. Build me a skin

of glass to cover the Grand Canyon,
throw me on it. Summon a thousand wilding mares,
restrain them with massive chains, foot-long links

of hardened steel. When the chains buck
from fracture, let the mares stampede the glass,
bid them trample my body.

Watch, from a great distance, as the glass cracks.
Watch us beasts entangle. Watch me take a hoof
to the mouth. To the skull. To the groin.

Hear us squeal, and bark, and howl,
calling out, as wretches do, to failing life.

When at last we one thousand and one blood-filled creatures
reach the bottom of the Canyon, throw yourself in.
My voice in your ear will tell you that you were meant to die

like this, a beautiful and inelegant dive onto a field of reds,
some bright and sun-kissed, some dark and pulp-dashed,
your and our blood across the burnt-orange schist.

See, O, see what I have done.
I fear neither the sight of nor the word for *blood*.
HMAS Albatross has joined the search for the plane.

It is May now, and there is no sign of it.
The detritus lied. The home I made is of orchids,
forsythia, barbed wire, and burnt metal.

In the bedroom I planted what I imagine
a midnight tree to be. Its roots join the treeless roots

in the armory beneath. Ravished, my hands cut off,
my tongue cut out, I put my home under the wisteria,
craving owls at war under thick purple overhang.

No territory there is that is not mine.
The Albatross, it is mine.
Enceladus is mine. Your innermost thigh,

beneath the wisteria, mine.
Poseidon is mine, and the river between Boston and Cambridge,
and the one that wends through Georgia, floods

into the Gulf. I am dreaming of a monument
to moments colonized by theaters of the imagination.
O monstrous. The O of a mouth without a tongue.

The O of two pairs of lips clasped,
starving on one another. Horns and cry of hounds.

The ballet in my deadly standing eye
is the arrow's flight into the neck, the horses' tumble into the canyon.
A nation's search for a single tiger

with quills in its neck. A spilt cloud of felled bees.
The elephant's horror in the flock of red-billed birds,
feathered locusts who from their first breath

form trembling caverns with their mouths, their aggregate force
snapping branches off trees. The orchestra plays low drumbeats,
a single singer carving the melody.

Do not, I pray, promise me
an untroubled lake. Take me instead
to the rivers with vengeful gods

under steaming and frozen waters.
Take me instead for the stag, the rifle, and the hunter.

Promise me unending days in which I can picture,
then picture again, a fire whirl,
the slowness of the sea drinking

a ferry or a plane, the gasps of air bubbles
around carapaces, the moons of Saturn.
I myself am hells, and I prize them

as if they were the rarest blooms.
Promise me I will always reach again for spears,
await the horses on the glass

above the gaping, hollow O of the earth.
ALL IS LOST. FLEE THIS HOUSE.
So chants James's Ouija.

or perhaps in the palace of time
our lives are a circular stair and i am turning,

writes Lucille's ghost-guided hand. Always in my mouth
I hold the head of an axe with its bit at the back
of my throat. O heavens, can you hear a man groan?

Here nothing breeds but we fazed and hungry. O wondrous thing.
Worlds such as this were not thought possible to exist,
writes the astronomer. It is June.

Deep beneath those golden waves
of the river I'll be found.
My sister has joined the list of those I mourn.

Her ghost lives in each powder-winged moth.
In the ballet, the stage fills with a troupe of dancers in dusty gold skirts,
shoes asphyxiation blue, hair the tones of flesh.

Center stage are six dancers who wear only red,
moving in unison

so they throb as one bloodied yolk.
The troupe around them shudders
as though in blissful death throes.

The single singer quiets. The orchestra
breaks down its instruments.
For my brethren slain

I ask a sacrifice,
O barbarous, beastly villains
like myself.

Die. Die saying *please*,
die longing, die helpless,
die with your eyes fixed

to the most treacherous side
of a mountain, to newborn stars,

to planes not found.
Die with your throat stuffed,
so that each moment hereafter

is a dream of a gasp.
Die, so that my midnight tree might grow
new branches, die, like a sapling struck by lightning

in an ash-ridden and still smoldering field,
die amid the tulips, die smelling the orchids I grow,
die in the mass of horses in a pied flock of shrieking birds.

From the oceans creatures great and small
take to the land. From the land
each parachuted seed

takes to the sky.
From within my armory

comes a scent melodious and unearthly.
A strain of moths, black, flies as though sewn
each to each at the wing. Their flight path

blooms dark into the gray air
like a print from a silvered glass plate.
Soon we will learn our bodies are formed

of dead stars, so that if we made incisions
from breastbone to rectum, the caves within
would reveal themselves to house celestial ash.

As the stag, I fear the mouth of the rifle.
As the rifle, I point my mouth, deadly, toward you.
As the hunter, I execute myself so I may feast.

Worlds such as this were not thought possible to exist.
My lord, I aim a mile beyond the honeyed moon.

MOST OF THE CHILDREN WHO LIVED IN THIS
HOUSE ARE DEAD. AS A CHILD I LIVED HERE.
THEREFORE I AM DEAD.

Figure 1. What takes place after the death of animals.

> After the dogs were buried beneath the patch of blue pansies, their ghosts
> took up residence in the black upright piano in the drawing room of the
> house. The moon came up, and the pollen stopped falling. It had already
> fallen on the dandelions, the grasses, two girls and a woman and a man,
> and the blue pansies. When the pollen stopped, the house looked like a
> butterflied breast. Nearby was a stadium, where improbably graceful men
> invented new kinds of physics.

Figure 2. A museum, cherished, which was once a home, and imagined as such.

> At a different house, two lions guarded a tiled courtyard filled with
> hurricane plants, also called *Monstera deliciosa*. The lions were stone.
> There were flights of stairs in the courtyard that led to spaces, like the
> Blue Room, from which you could survey the courtyard from above. The
> spaces were full of artifacts and tapestries, and one of the girls went there
> often to learn the meaning of *house*. The lions were owned by a woman
> who took them on long walks through the stone-paved city.

Figure 3. Apostrophe to the reader.

> I am not writing this poem as a fable because I am afraid to speak of
> myself. I am writing it as a fable because I am afraid to speak of you, by
> which I mean that I suspect that some of these things may have happened
> to you also, and I am concerned that you will not hear that unless I make
> for you a fiction. Of course, I am also egotistical enough to think that
> I can speak of you if I use generalities, and to suppose that any of the
> houses I have been in are the same as those from which your night terrors
> originate.

Figure 4. What led to the death of animals.

Next to the black upright piano was a window, which looked out at the blue pansies, which were also sometimes purple, or yellow, like the word *contusion.* Near the patch was an oak that was once encircled by weeks' worth of shit, and a chain that once encircled one dog's neck. Next to the window was a medicine cabinet. The other dog used to sit next to it. The fish met a swift end with a gallon of bleach. A child is being beaten, as is another, and a woman.

Figure 5. One of the children visits the museum.

Around the courtyard there were—and still are, because this house, unlike the other, has not been overtaken by walls of bees—cloisters. In the cloisters are sarcophagi and living statues. The girl wrote: *In the end, you will inherit only the finest silence, or the darkest retreat.* In the sarcophagus next to the bench toward which the lovers who visit the courtyard are partial, children hide: *Look at me. Look at me. I'm dead.* The girl, who had by then spent fifteen years as a connoisseur of grammars of violence, said little.

Figure 6. Early lessons in physics and metaphysics.

When the other dog died, he was bluer than the pansies. Particularly his gums. That is how the girl learned that death need not involve a chain to be the product of force. That is also when the girl began to learn the words *psychopath* and *sociopath* in the English language. The distinction quickly confused her, and she learned that this confusion is not the product of language acquisition, but rather one of many brief genealogies of a characteristic aspect of human beings.

Figure 7. Rebellion against physics and metaphysics.

Which is to say: the inability to look at cruelty and accurately name it; or, the inability to look at cruelty without needing to try to name it. Here is what none of the dictionaries or lexica will be able to fully accommodate: every time the girl played the black upright piano, the man who also lived in the house thought, *How wonderful it is that the ghosts of the dogs have learned to sing, and how fortunate it is there are a range of art forms that can prepare bodies for their journey toward the river dark.*

Figure 8. Apostrophe to the reader.

I am also writing this poem as a fable because at times I *have* been afraid to speak of myself, and lately it has become important to me to learn how to respect that my earliest affections for abstraction were by way of disguise, that my turn next to straightforwardness was by way of retaliation, and that I will always negotiate between the two like a brown, black-haired Goldilocks, perpetually dissatisfied with the size of the offering, although now, I tend to think of obstruction and clarity alike as acts of definition.

Figure 9. A lover's discourse.

In one of the rooms in the museum was a painting of Europa lying on a bull, feeling what the girl at the time thought to be love, for the simple reasons that Europa's thighs were spread, and one of her legs was curled, and her head was thrown back and her mouth open, and she seemed to be holding fiercely onto one of the horns of the bull, who wore a garland and looked straight at the viewer, and because the sky, in the background, held glimmers of salmon-pink, and the water nearby seemed a greenish blue.

Figure 10. To the reader.

I am also writing this poem as a fable because it is my sense that the emotional impact of the genre owes a great deal to the fact that what counts as *denouement* is instead a reiteration of the text's limitations, which is to say that a fable never *resolves* so much as re-declares its problems, while all the same insinuating that such re-declaration can pass, seductively, as a tale of progress. Here is an explication by way of analogy: the earliest version of this book took as its climax my sister's death, which is now its beginning.

Figure 11. New forms of physics and metaphysics.

Most of the children who lived in this house are dead. As a child I lived here. Therefore I am dead. Most of the animals who lived in this house are dead. As an animal I lived here. Therefore I am dead. The English word *planet* comes from ancient Greek and Latin words meaning *wander* or *wanderer*. As children and animals we live on a planet. Therefore we wander and are wanderers. The alphabets, essentially, are trees. Therefore this book is a forest. No forest is ever a forest alone.

QUIVER

Speak to me never again about sacrifice.

Tell me no stories about things left behind.

Should you dream of telling me such a thing

Imagine immediately yourself in front of Orpheus.

Know that for the rest of my life

I do and will name everything Eurydice,

No matter what else I pretend I have named it.

I do not know what my own eyes look like

But often I imagine them like the eyes of a hound

Fresh from the track.

The track, too, is Eurydice.

Each lover. Three dogs. Rose bushes.

My mother, my sister, my home state.

An underground bees' nest. One upright black Kawai piano.

Here are the words you may not speak to me

Because I know them better than you could:

Toil. Sacrifice. Hound. Eurydice.

O SPIRIT

To help myself rise in the morning, I make a promise.

Someday, I will cause as much pain as I feel.

O SPIRIT

I have not been able to build the etymology of *love*.

The word, in its weight, is an eclipse.

O SPIRIT

I no longer love.

To prove this, I have cut off my hands.

NIGHT QUESTIONS

When does the moon turn full?

When I tell it stories of love.

When does the moon begin to wane?

When I stop speaking of love.

What do you look like in the dark?

A horned, lit, and petrified tree on a shore.

To whom do you turn when in pain?

DEAR, BELOVED

Child. We are done for
in the most remarkable ways.
— BRIGIT PEGEEN KELLY, *"Dead Doe"*

It would be winter, with a thin snow. An aged sunbeam
would fall on me, then on a nearby summit, until a mass
of ice would appear like a crown of master diamonds
in shades of gold and pink. The base of the mountains
would be still in darkness. The snow would melt,
making the mountain uglier. The ice would undertake
a journey toward dying. My iliacus, from which orchids bloom,
would learn to take an infant's shape, some premature creature
weaned too soon. My femoral nerve, from which lichen grows
in many shades, would learn to take breaths of its own
and would issue a moan so labored it could have issued
from two women carrying a full-length wooden casket, with dirt
made from a girl inside. The dirt would have been buried
with all of the girl's celestial possessions. Bearing the casket
would demand more muscles than earthbound horses have.
The girl would have been twenty-four. This was my *visio.*
Sometimes I think of it as prophecy. Other times, history.
For years it was akin to some specific land, with a vessel
that would come for me, able to cross land, sea, the spaces
of the universe, able to burrow deep into the ground.
Anything could summon it—a breaking in cloud cover,
wind chimes catching salt outside my mother's window,
a corner of a painting. And I learned how to call it, too.
This is the only skill of which I have ever been proud.
When my sister died, from the head of my visio came offspring
in the thousands, armed to the teeth, each its own vessel.
My first, their mother, lived on. For itself and its hoard

it found a permanent home in a cave at the bottom of a lake.
And it waited until I was standing on a mountain to sing to me:
You will call this mountain home until I tell you to move again.
There will always be more of it underground than you
will ever see with your eye. And so it turned out to be true.
And so when I stood on the mountain that became my home,
I beheld a dirt sea, and I saw our moon, which has two faces.
I learned that one face of our moon is dappled with maria,
and that the sunbeams here are newborns that lie
on each other, purpling into the fog and outstretched pines.
Earth spins masses of air until it looks like one of the many
irises studding our galaxy. From space, parts of the Atlantic
look like leather, wrinkled and dark, and others look
like iridescent fishes in an Old Master's painting of the sky.
I live in the valley of a crater here, where steam rises like ghosts
in the summer heat. This mountain is made of igneous stone.
Every day I issue a warning to lovers: Darlings, I have
in my possession a dead girl deer. Her head is draped
over my right shoulder. I hold her with one arm
encircling her torso. You wake each morning with flowers
shrouding your body, like a corpse; I put them there.
To me, you died when my legs curved around your head.
One of the deer's eyes has blackened, and her tongue is thick.
She belonged to my sister. O my sister, you were twenty-four.
Listen close. Even to this part. Especially this.
I want you to hear what I say to lovers, because I want to sing
to you, who died a virgin, a few treatises on love and sex—
how flesh and ecstasy are born, what they make,
how they live out their days. As a bodied girl
you feared me, and I met your fear with guttural disdain.
I imagine you wondered what it would take for me to hear
a mortal, human voice: whenever you spoke, a vessel came
for me, chattering like some frail and hissing bird,
pigeon-chested, thin-veined feet. Sister, I don't listen to lovers,
either, who I call by the same names that were yours:
dear, beloved. But spirits are not like their progenitors.
Their touches can range from velvet to bristle.

Lover, each time I kiss you I name after you
a sickly feeling in my own body, as if each ailing
is a previously undiscovered moon orbiting a planet
that can only sustain the strangest of life-forms.
Sister, I know neither goodness nor mercy shall follow me
all the days of my life, as surely as I know the beasts
I inherit or create, of all unions familial or otherwise,
are speechless and brute, and bound to die soon.
Yes, there is much to love about the body.
Too, there is much to hate. I cast off care for pleasure,
and for labor, teaching my body over time that these things
can't coexist. I fear it has started to believe me.
My body has never sought wholeness the way yours did, sister.
It was always still the dull twilight of early morning with us.
You were twenty-four, and when you died, I stopped fearing
arson. When I picture us as girls, we are at the base
of the mountain from my visio, divining the summit
as we diminish into spots of light. We are without parentage.
On my mountaintop in midafternoons flocks of wheeling
birds gather around the crescent moon. When the moon
worms its way through the clouds, it fixes its eyes on me
and sings a song that says we live our lives chained to earth,
and that when we die the flesh falls off our bones
so our bones can turn into the driest of riverbed dirt.
Sister, when you died, your bones cast an enchantment.
We made a powder of them, and I named the powder *ash*,
because *ash* is a word with neither origin nor afterlife,
and its definition is the look a doe gets when she's been away
from her herd too long. When a person goes missing
and we don't know her name, we grant her the surname *Doe*.
With this christening we name all missing persons
part of the family of *ash*, which has no family.
Sometimes I think that each speck of *ash*
previously named *Priya* hums on quiet nights
in a frequency only the other pieces can hear.
Inaudible to the waking world she hums to herself.
That hum is how my blood became blue; in lieu of oxygen,

my body began to breathe in only the vibrations of the hum.
Blood has to be born into its colors. Or, more precisely,
it has to die into them. In Hesiod's *Theogony*, Nyx is born
of Chaos. Erebus, Gaia, and Tartarus are her siblings.
Hesiod couldn't decide whether Nyx birthed the Fates
or whether the Fates were born of someone else, but he knew
that Nyx's children, whoever they were, had no sire.
About Nyx's brothers and sisters, Hesiod writes:
Earth too, and great Oceanus, and dark Night,
the holy race of all the other deathless ones that are for ever,
and one day—what? Tell me. Tell me the song they taught you.
Tell me how you learned how beautiful Nyx is,
how you realized Zeus feared her, and how you first saw
that within her every star, from the swollen to the hollow,
from the living to the dead, is visible, powered by little
but her peerless face. When I returned north for the first time
since my father turned my sister into a powder named *ash*,
a word born of nothing and with no children, I heard her
from a seagull on the ferry I rode from the harbor to the Cape,
out of a piping plover on the dunes, in a crow's call on the highway
from Boston to Gloucester, past Folly Cove, Prides Crossing,
Rust Island. Then, from my station again on the mountain,
I heard my own voice from a brown thrasher. That night I drove
through remains of a fresh accident on the mountain highway.
The dropping sun lit my back as if heralding fire.
A dislocated red front bumper straddled the median,
singing a song. Nyx was in the wind, and her siblings,
and they bade me sing, too, like Hesiod had asked.
Grant lovely song, celebrate the holy race of the deathless
gods who are for ever, born of Earth and starry Heaven
and gloomy Night and them that briny Sea did rear.
Soon all were singing. The median sang with the deep voice
of a woman who knows how to sing scat, and the mountain,
standing like a moon on Earth, responded with a wordless song
of its own creation. Ash sang. Dirt sang. To them I lent a melody,
which is one of the things I do when I can't sleep. The secret
about lullabies: when they work, it's because they sound

like something plants would sing in Hades, on the banks
of the river dark. Oh how I wish they worked on me.
When the sculptor couldn't sleep, she drew mountains.
They were pink, red, ridged and pulsing, and rose
from valleys of blue. Or else she'd draw eyes that held
too many irises, or wombs that bore cysts,
or spindle-legged women with outsized, drooping breasts,
ill-formed and misshapen eyes for nipples, uneven halos
for areolae, made of the same skin as the kind under eyes
that have been open for too long. Those songs I sing
when I can't sleep are directed to my army of visios.
In return, they give me images of myself as different
creatures: gibbons, a chicken with a plucked-feather neck,
an asteroid, a mountain, a volcano with the thinnest
and most translucent shell. Me, as some fantastical beast with eyes
lining the inside of my body, watching my diaphragm
turn into the ocean I saw from the ferry, watching plumes of sun
flare over it as it comes to resemble a dead animal's
long-weathered skin. Ghostly ships with dropped anchors
materialize to trawl it, and squadrons of men dismount,
searching for new blooms in terra mountainous and lush.
My heart is a sky embalmed and bright. When the phantoms
drop anchor, there to welcome their sailors are screaming pelicans
on the rocks, and parades continually wheeling of ugly vultures
in funereal garb. In their eyes, the Atlantic always looks besieged
by hurricane. *Lunar maria* means *moon seas*, but when I hear it
I picture horses, torqued female beasts who live on the moon
and whose manes are made of the roots of moon-trees.
I did not want to die, but I wanted to want death.
None of you ever knew how badly. I have practiced at it.
At times I rehearsed like a dancer, surrounded by mirrored walls.
At others I moonlighted with movies set on battlefields
and in abattoirs, pausing and rewinding until I could mimic
the motions of actresses who succumb to unexpected poison,
or shove knives into their bellies, or fall like Brueghel's boy.
I pretended I was standing in a castle dressed like a samurai,
looking through a barred window, knowing the trees

approaching held a promise so annihilative my flesh
would have no choice but to accept. I pictured jumping
from the top of the mountain and I sang *Love it Love it Love it.*
On my mountain the birds shroud the pines, and the pines
make a spectral outline against the valley of Nyx's body.
One afternoon here a man said to his son: *All this has to do*
with eons of time, water over and over, just cutting and cutting
the rock. From where I stand on its summit, I can touch
the Big Dipper and I can see its children, and another peak,
shaped like the back of a horse. It is shadow blue, the same blue
as the dying sky. To the Big Dipper and her children I sing a song
that asks if they are safe, and tells them that on forest floors,
dappled things of glass and light grow from knotted roots.
Sister, could I find you on that horse mountain? I wonder
if I want to. Have I made this world? Lover, a confession.
If I found my sister on any mountain, I would gather her
in my arms and take her from its back, singing lullabies.
Or else I'd take an arrow laced with a drug I'd made special
for her, and, standing close, push it in her unarmed
right flank. Instead of how to die, I ended up studying
how to kill. But the sculptor, she asked nothing of her dead.
Out of visions of them she made formidable metal spiders
she named *Maman, Maman, Maman. Maman Maman Maman,*
who live after the sculptor has died, have all lost children,
like my mother. Their domains are terrors—land-terrors,
water-terrors, terrors of the open sky. Their hearts are war-
grief. Terrors of trees in the joyless forest, of portent.
Sometimes in their homes are fires on floods, dire wonders.
Their children were all named *Doe,* which means that the plural
form for children of *Maman* is *deer.* For a long time I hated
the phrase *I am sorry for your loss.* I *lost* nothing. My sister *died.*
But *loss* is less of a euphemism than its users imagine it to be;
to lose means both *to have been defeated* and *to misplace.*
Maman Maman Maman also answers to *Demeter Demeter Demeter.*
Sister, I could stop no one from taking your head,
although I promise you I fought for it, hand-to-hand
by the mouth of the bone-house. One day on my mountain,

I got to thinking about those other peaks. From a cave
underwater I heard: *Find them, like flowers strange
and never before seen.* And so it became true.
I found mountains covered in smoke-thick fogs,
and mountains that lied—those were barely hills.
And then I found them: what the mountains in my visio
would have looked like had it been summer in that land.
Summer brought some changes: my body had no orchids
or lichen, and the crown was not of diamonds, but the reek
of sewage, wafting over a field—a prairie almost—
from which rose tens of signal towers, all blinking red.
The base of mountains was, when I got there, still,
and in darkness. It was a sky in which every child of every star,
living or dead, could be heard humming. The peerless
face of the mountain was cragged rock, dust rock, shadow rock.
I stayed until day, to watch the birth of a sunbeam
so I could then see it age. Later in the day an immense heat
came, like another bone-house. I climbed the ridges, which turned
to colored ringlets of cloud and ash at the slightest pressure.
Sunrise and sunset were scant minutes of shadow play.
The prairie grass's rustle, each blade sang in a different language.
There I learned the names of four of the lunar mares:
Catfire, Osiris, Blood Oath, and Early Morning.
This is who I am. I harbor secret loves, and I do secret work.
Catfire, Osiris, Blood Oath, and Early Morning are teaching me
how to finally chart a course through time, how to carve
journeys in space: they descended from their moon to the crags,
followed me home to my moonlike mountain. Lover, my body—
you won't be able to keep up with it. Soon you'll have to leave it.
You'll have to leave me. Or else I'll leave you, because my body,
it invents definitions for the word *sadness*, like *noun, the feathers
on a bird's back.* You'll do nothing for me. On my mountain,
it's midafternoon, and the wheeling birds are landing
steadily, even though no stable ground is here to be found.
When they sing, it is a song that I, who know no prayers,
imagine to be gospel. A man comes up the mountainside
and sings along with them as he walks in circles on the rock.

Robbed, sister, was your breath. Robbed, lover, is yours, too.
Sister, I wish you could know this feeling: if sung perfectly,
pressure on each nerve cluster can make bones irrelevant, whether
those bones are living or dead, whether they are ash or dirt.
At the base of my mountain is a lake where creatures go to die.
Water slides into their spiracles and fills their tracheae.
Their tracheae stretch into bellows fit to extinguish the fires
in any volcano. When my body showed me *sadness*
and began there to outline and diagram the word,
another definition was *noun, a chorus of brass instruments,*
like upward-turned mouths forged of metal, and another was *verb,*
to shake like chimes flanking a rock-hewn shore, barely alive
and almost imperceptible for a flash. Sometimes I picture
my sister underneath one of the sculptor's spiders.
Her head barely reaches the first joint on the spider's leg,
and when she looks up, she thinks that the whole sky
is the spider's stomach. *Maman,* she says, *I am hungry.*
Food. Food. I am hungry. She runs her shrunken finger
from one tagma to another. Her stroke makes lava run faster
in all the volcanoes within the tectonic plate on which she lives,
and she, unawares, suckles at every ridge she can find.
She rests both palms flat against the metal, closes her eyes
and cries. What would the world look like with enough lava
to fill the Atlantic? I know that Earth's temperature
has risen, and I know that all of its ice will melt.
I know there will be no more purple from the sun, that the spider's
iron underside is one of the few things that, like my mother,
does not sing. At the lake today is a flock of feral cats.
Though they're in front of me, their song comes from below,
so although I can see them, I picture them swimming in a river
that separates mortals from the planet's heart. In this river floats
the phantom of a dead doe. Listen to me now, darlings:
my sister did not live long enough to see the moon
turn red, but I did, and despite those who wish otherwise,
myself included, I will see it again. *Sadness*'s fourth definition
is *conjunction, bees, forests of them, devotional and thick enough*
to knot together human dreams, or human bodies, even when ghostly,

or lovelorn. The underground river gives me no passage,
despite my dreams of the phantom that dropped anchor
somewhere, and of its amassed pelicans and vultures.
Each ghost is filled to the brim with flowers whose scents
describe the places they were born, just like mine does,
no matter how hard I try to cloak it. On the top of my mountain
a man says to a woman: *I like how there's just trees. Trees trees trees,*
she replies. Each time she says the word, her voice makes
a new species. I recently tried another way to die: could I fall
from a tower filled wall-to-wall with twenty-four thousand
living flowers, each planted in the soil covering the tower's floors,
six inches deep? The flowers would have heavy-branched
spikes for blooms, and would release a powerful smell
of bone marrow, and spew a pollen that fills the air until
it becomes oppressive. When I opened my mouth to sing
of this, instead of a sound my mouth expelled gnats and fog,
which is what a spider's milk is made of. The word *Nyx*
tastes like *sister* and means both *night* and *flower*. I worry
I won't rest again. Do you know how a naked Titan looks,
sister? He's swarmed with shadow, but he holds light deep
in his stomach, like an electric secret. Dear love,
I can't give you what you need from me. All I'll do is take.
After my sister died, I learned she always wanted a warm island,
garlands draped around her neck. There was no mountain
in her vision. Instead, in it she was singing what she imagined
was an island song in a language I don't know. She was dancing
badly, and breathing with great labor on burnished sands.
Sand bores me, sister; I need rock and high altitude.
When I am cold, I hear wolves. I think they live in the carillon
beside the mountain's lake. Sister, it was always true
that I would outlive you. I know exactly how many times
my family wished me dead. *Don't look up,* says a child
on the top of my mountain. *It makes you want to fall.*
It will always be still the dull twilight of early morning with us.
This is one of the curses of living. In the end, my visio alone
will sing and dance, breathing heavily. Every day the sunbeams
in it turn a brighter pink. Dears. Beloveds. All of you.

Your blood is bewitched, and bade to move into places
it wasn't meant to go, steeped deeply in poisons
it can't purge. You share the look on your face
with all the others, whether deer, child, or man.
If you look deeply enough into any other pair of eyes,
your heart valves start to change allegiances. Your body's lakes
fill with the other's want, until all you want, in turn,
is what the other wants, which rises in you like seawater.
There are species of flowers and invasive weeds that live only
in another's gaze, whether lovelorn, hate-filled, hopeless,
or hungry. I am looking into your eyes right now,
and in my mind are two girl deer. Sisters. With thin-hooved
legs steady, digging into grass. They disappear into the woods,
which are part of a forest in a painting. When the novelist
saw this painting, he thought that there he could see men
turning into birds and birds turning into men,
and those same men turning then into sea creatures,
and then back into birds. From this final change
scales and tentacles would linger on their backs
as they wheeled through the air, as would the dream
of filling their lungs with the sea, for which they would ache.
The definition of *deer* is *lost*. The definition of *beloved*
is *dissolution*. On the top of my mountain I hear a mother
call to a faceless child, *Where are you?* The chattering
and thin voice of a boy from the top of a tree cries back,
In the woods. And then, beguilingly: *Come into the woods.*
Around the orbs of light in the forest that I still don't know
if the Dipper's children can see, new trees grow beside the pines:
elms, birches, willows, one strange western juniper.
Each creature in this forest was once something, or someone, else—
the novelist was right. The top of one of the elms
is a sprig of radiant blood. Sister, I was very young
when I found out you were cloven-hoofed. I did what I could.
I want to say that you can trust me, that I am listening to you,
and that you can speak to me and that I will speak to you
at last. Tell me about the beasts that got you. The beasts
who carry me when I am too weak to carry my deer alone

are Catfire, Osiris, Blood Oath, and Early Morning.
I would like to believe that I carry this deer for you,
that I'll be able to tell you what it feels like to have
a hungry mouth on your lip or nipple. I want to say:
Sister, I promise. But the definition of *myth* is *noun,*
the idea that any one creature can ever hear another.
And while I beguile you to betray yourself to me,
like lovers do in their sleep, I am lying to you. No, death
did not bring this to us. It has always been true. I, sister,
am a selfish woman, and you, sister, were a mute one.
My body invents words and swells with prophecies.
Its effort shows in insect bites and rashes that don't heal,
in my peeled hands, bleeding groin, wistful gut, misaligned jaw,
mole-like left eye, lump-riddled womb. Dears. Beloveds.
You've been asleep a long time, but we all return
to the waking world someday. And when you do at last
come back, you will find me spent and alone, ugly,
wounded, ungrateful, ill. Shaking and calling to you for aid.
Loveless. Without a soul or even the memory of pleasure.
The last lover to desert me will deem me rancid.
The last thing I hear my sister's voice from will be dirt.
Of the mares I will have left only Early Morning,
who won't know that I will soon take her hide,
turn it into an ocean that will, at last, cleave open my skull.

O SPIRIT

A bear brings forth her young informous and unshapen.

I now wear the pelt of the conjured beast around my groin.

I think of new words for *solace*, one of which is *knifed*.

We take no form until licked into shape by the tongues of those who love us.

O SPIRIT

It takes work for a woman to welcome a fist
With her body. Fists are larger than the spaces

They make for themselves in a chest, or the holes
Into which we welcome them with longing.

Asking whether I wish for one now because I knew
Them well as a child is like asking if a volcano

Expels lava because, when a small mountain
Cloistered within seawaters, its first experience

Of heat was unbidden. The question
Requires a certain old knowledge of safety to ask.

What does it mean that the first time you saw a cock
It was raised in menace from a boil of shared blood,

The question says. *Tell me the origin story of pain,*
And tell me what happens to pain as it ages,

And tell me how the ocean-bottom dirt you grew
From tastes. Volcanoes understand differences

In kinds and in chords. The origin story of pain
Is abjection, foisted. Not a single stream of lava

Is like one that has come before or will come since.
All my lips make treacherous lights float in midair.

O SPIRIT

Of Moby-Dick

I wish to lay before you
a particular, plain statement
whose skeleton we are
briefly to exhibit
out of the trunk,
the branches grow, out of them,
the twigs
chased over the watery
moors, slaughtered
in the valleys—oil and bone
pass unscathed through the fire
and it is only
gray imperfect misty dawn,
soon we shall be lost
in its unshored, harborless
immensities that serene
ocean rolled eastwards from me
a thousand leagues of blue and I only
am escaped alone to tell thee
only I am escaped to tell thee.

BASIC QUESTIONS

What was the experience of death like for you?

The fluids within my body failed to be held within my body, which, as far as I can tell, does not entirely differ from some experiences of life,

At what moment did you know there was an existence beyond earth?

as when, for example, I lay beneath another's beautiful body of my own free will for the first time and learned in one of those staggering moments that I had hairs within my nostrils,

How did you feel?

because they stood on end, as if confused by which hole was meant to receive the body that was on top of me,

Were you met by anyone?

rapt into confusion. I once got to see inside of my own lower abdomen. Did you know there is a galaxy there? I have photographs to prove it.

What things in our world still attract you most?

My veins make azalea roots that teem with messages. There are lights whose names I don't know. Malignancies are moons. There's gold on the ocean shores. Planets made of other planets, growing into one another to rewrite the old rules about space and about time. I saw it all, through the eye within the eye. Someday, I'll show you.

What would you like to clarify for our world about your life?

Daily existence, mine included, was nothing short of improbable.

Do you wish to return again?

Foucault once wrote, "The venomous heart of things and men is, at bottom, what I've always tried to expose."

Is there a message you would like to give to our world?

Rilke once wrote, "You must change your life."

Is there anything that you wouldn't mind saying that would help assure your friends that you are you?

Whatever I have loved, I have taken its name in vain.

ESSAY ON THE ORDER OF TIME

On the mountain a man said to his son, *All this has to do with eons of time, water over and over, just cutting and cutting the rock.* While the verb most often associated with *eons of time* is *to cut,* as to the ever-present question of when the mountain was first born and how it will die, that is not about cutting but rather about *swell,* specifically that of magma. At both its birth and its eventual death, the mountain's temporality is unfixed, by which I mean it is both ongoing and conclusive.

Here is an explication by way of analogy. I am composed of cysts that are made of dead blood. If they are excised, they return. If a hole is cracked into one and the blood spooned out, the shell will refill. Not all of them will always be made of dead blood. At least one will turn into rock, and that will be the one that will need at all costs to be scaled and defaced. It will then become something new, and, if the alteration is successful, it will become the same as what it once was.

In *The Order of Things,* Foucault writes that *man is an invention of recent date. And one perhaps nearing its end . . . one can certainly wager that man would be erased, like a face drawn in sand at the edge of the sea.* This statement is not unlike *All this has to do with eons of time, water over and over, just cutting and cutting the rock.* They are most similar in cadence and rhythm, which in both phrases balance surety with spectral doubt. One of their main differences: Foucault's accommodates magma, and strange time.

The original title of *The Order of Things* is *Les mots et les choses,* or *Words and Things.* The substitution of *Order* for *Words* speaks to one of our most pervasive myths, that words have a clear order. A similar myth underwrites the substitution of *and* with *of,* as though there is an orderly kingdom of syntax conducive to organizational subordination. Here is an explication by way of experiment: imagine the man's phrase, but replace *of* with *and*: *All this has to do with eons and time.*

This idea that there is an *order of things* often reveals its illusory nature, particularly when the conversation turns to death. For example, in the edition I own of T. J. Clark's *The Sight of Death,* many of the captions for images of Poussin's *Landscape with a Man Killed by a Snake* are erroneously punctuated. Some of them end with commas in lieu of periods, and at least one ends with nothing, rendered as "Detail of *Landscape with a Man Killed by a Snake*"

All of the other captions are end-stopped, like so: "Detail of *Landscape with a Calm*." Albeit presumably unintentional, the insinuation is that calm produces a discrete end, whereas there is no border for death or its sightings. This feels loosely analogous to Foucault's decision to title his book, which ends with the disappearance of man, *Les mots et les choses*. In both cases, however, the myth is so strong that its counterargument vanishes, or is termed errata, like a cyst.

The opposite insinuation is made in the following story, which I first heard from a man at the end of a performance of a violin concerto: after a beloved dies, one must lock the door to one's house. One must seal in the ghost. Here, the argument is that death requires the most discrete borders of all things, and that there is a clear order to how it functions as an event in time. The concerto was being performed in honor of a poet who had recently died. To face this loss, this man required the myth of order.

Experiment, continued: *Just cutting of cutting the rock, sand at the edge and the sea, water over of over*. The face of sand leaves the beach. The currents carry it elsewhere, depositing it on another sandbank as an object lesson in the borderless nature of death. And so in that elsewhere, in another shape, a face of sand is rearranged into a dune, or a cliff, or a mountain, some structure so seemingly harmless that even children think it is there for them to climb.

ESSAY ON DEVOTION

Death, at least in one of Dürer's woodcuts, is a charming skeleton; he steadies a casket on his shoulder with one hand while the other hand seduces the Fool's robe. The woodcut can be found in the first *Ship of Fools* book and is called *Not Preparing for Death*. The Fool, at least as well as I can make out, is carrying a paper-wrapped bouquet of calla lilies.

It's an anachronism for me to claim the Fool holds calla lilies, since the lily was "discovered" in the eighteenth century, and Dürer came from a previous time, a time before the West had invented for them this name. Calla lilies are one of my mother's favorite kinds of flower, which is why, when I picture this charming skeleton come to pick up my sister, I imagine also a nearby Fool, holding calla lilies.

Here are some of my favorite lines of poetry, made with some of my other favorite lines of poetry: *Stevens wrote that // For a poem to be true, it must "come from an Ever." / If you don't fathom that, then you should not be reading this.* These lines are intended to forbid, which is a less cherished and equally indispensable impulse as that of invitation. *Ever* is not a place; *to fathom* means *to measure what cannot be measured.*

I imagine *Ever* the way I imagine *Elsewhere:* the *thousand-armed river* down which the Ship of Fools sailed, the *great uncertainty that surrounds all things*. To agree with the above means, then, to permit two facts: that it is not possible for a poem to exist, and that to read a poem is to embark on a mission that bears no bloom. Both facts mean that in the business of poetry, you are Death's Fool, with an armful of calla lilies.

My agreement with these lines is therefore both a form of self-love and one of self-loathing, for I too have a ship, although I cannot fathom much, and my ship itself is not fit to sail a thousand-armed river. My ship is also not a poem, by which I mean both that my ship exists and, at the same time, that it is not *true*, which I understand to mean *faithful*. It is an exercise in failure.

ESSAY ON THUNDER

A woman made wary by misfortune, writes Stendhal, *will not experience this soul-shaking upheaval. Soul-shaking upheaval* means something like what he elsewhere calls *the curse of passionate love,* although my sense is that *love* here is better understood as either *arousal* or *torpor,* and that distinctions in such matters are, while necessary and true, ultimately mythological. Stendhal's own argument also entails a critique of terminology: of *thunderbolts,* he says, *That ridiculous word ought to be changed—but nevertheless the thing "love at first sight" does exist.*

When I first copied down those sentences from Stendhal, I wrote instead of *upheaval* the nonword *unheaval,* which I now think of as *upheaval*'s uncompromised sibling. On the ceiling of my gynecologist's exam room is a watercolor of a lurid hummingbird with a few centimeters of beak inside a flower. A hummingbird's beak is understood to be a sheath for the bird's tongue, which means the tongue is a knife. Hummingbirds use their beaks to feed, as well as to do battle. There has not yet been a study of what their tongues do in such times of war.

ESSAY ON JOY

When as a child my father deemed my weight excessive, the measure of which shifted according to whim, he would take his underwear off of his body and place it on top of my head. I was to run in circles around the house, wearing it, for a prescribed number of times. This was called "exercise."

I am undertaking a new labor: I will imagine myself into deep, focused, and strange hatreds. Spinoza writes, *He who imagines that what he hates is destroyed will rejoice.* Some years ago, dozens of grackles fell dead from the sky in Boston, the cause unknown. And so I think: *I detest grackles.* I rejoice.

If asked, I would have explained the cause: somewhere in a level of atmosphere for which humans hold no keys lived a green-shining carrion crow. As her name indicates, she ate dead bodies. But nothing had died there, ever; and so, she was hungry. She was kept company by this lack.

Sometimes, I tell myself that I cannot think of a lover with terribly much feeling at all. But this is a lie. The absence of feeling is an assertion of a feeling, and it is a memory, or an *exercise*, of a kind of joy I sometimes fear I have forgotten, because, as a lover, I have been slighted, and, as a child, often betrayed.

For some length of time that a crow considers painful and I cannot measure, she caressed her lack like a lover. But then she came to fear her lover, for it caused her pain, and she could not convince herself that she had no feeling for her lover. So she undertook an exercise of destruction and began to kill.

When as a child I turned to violence, my mother, who also feared my father and even more feared the thought that I might become him, tried to warn, *A fist is always made with four fingers that point back toward you.* This is the kind of thing a grackle would say, because on grackles' feet is one toe that always points backward.

Then the crow's fallow field of carrion was her new creation, and she had grown accustomed to hating the products of her own making. She ate some, and so she finally grew in size, and hated that, too. *She who imagines what she hates is destroyed will rejoice.* She opened a hole in the bottom of the atmosphere. Her kills fell.

WINDOWS

After Rilke's "Les Fenêtres"

I.

how much   loss
gains suddenly in emphasis
and   brilliant sadness

II.

far from that which lives and turns

III.

languages
of our vain comings and goings wilt and gnaw

IV.

beat them,   punish
them for having said and always said

V.

tear out, finally,   our spells

VI.

one life pours and grows impatient
for another life

VII.

     and the lovers, look on them there,
     immobile and frail
     pinned like the butterflies
     for the beauty of their wings

VIII.

          too great in the outdoors

IX.

     like the lyre, you should be
     rendered a constellation

X.

     like the scales or the lyre
     an almost-name of the ages' absences

XI.

       should I defend myself
     am I not intact

XII.

     one who loves is never   beautiful

XIII.

         tender – strained

XIV.

    all hazards are abolished
          at the middle of love
    with a little bit of space around it
    where we are the masters

XV.

    changeable like the sea

XVI.

    ice, sudden, where our face is mirrored
          traversed

XVII.

    taste of freedom compromised
    by the presence of fate

XVIII.

              for whom would I wait

XIX.

    with this heart all full which loss completes

XX.

    will I be found when the night abounds
    given over to you, inexhaustible

XXI.

    climb! turn far and away

XXII.

                                                    doubt
        that you can give the   excess which arrests me

XXIII.

                                        the sky: immense example
                    of depth and height

XXIV.

                    make of the air a round arena

XXV.

                    effort circumscribes
        our life enormous

XXVI.

        stretched toward the night

                        what

            escaped

XXVII.

                set   out in type on the page

                    a little

                image

            vague

XXVIII.

    like the greyhounds

                arranging their legs

XXIX.

    the sense of our rites

    waits

XXX.

    intent

XXXI.

          who rushes, who tilts, who remains
    after the abandonment of the night

XXXII.

         starry   avaricious

XXXIII.

    all the grand unbroken numbers
    that the night will multiply

XXXIV.

              new celestial youth

     the matutinal sky

XXXV.

    buckles   close

XXXVI.

    under the guise of tenderness

XXXVII.

    time   uses his jacket

XXXVIII.

    inconsolable space

XXXIX.

    turned me into wind,

    placed me in the river

XL.

    leaves   fled ...

XLI.

    I had drunk

    all of my abyss

XLII.

    one must not tire
    and eat with one's eyes

XLIII.

                vision watered
profusely a   garden of images

XLIV.

each bird whose flight crosses
my expanse

XLV.

nothing but looking seems like life to me

XLVI.

nothing but looking seems like life

XLVII.

while the prunes ripen
O my eyes, eaters of roses
you will drink the moon

XLVIII.

                I consent
and I consent   force

XLIX.

      oh   force
does not frighten me anymore, because it cradles me

L.

     in the morning, small wild,
               become almost a mouth
         all   worn and bloodless

LI.

     Be, stars, the rhymes
     found at the ends of end

LII.

          say *enough*

ARROW

Worlds such as this were not thought possible to exist.
— N A S A , *June 2, 2014*

Nyx.

Was it I who invaded the day, or the day who invaded me?
                    I do, I undo, I redo.
I enlarged the figure till it was a mountain—I don't fear the sublime—
                    and I cut off its head,
having already cut out its tongue. I have three siblings and flocks of children,
                    and though we're oft confused,
you must know that I differ from all: I am not my brother Darkness,
                    nor my sister Dirt, nor my brother Torment.
I am a time and I am an astronomy, a geometry I invented myself, an architecture,
                    a divine, and like any divine,
yes, I have made kin from unions with my kin. Out of a union with my brother
                    I made the nymphs,
the river and the boatsman, lullabies. If X is an obstruction,
                    and if the poetry of X was music,
then this poem is a musical obstruction, and if this poem is a musical obstruction,
                    then this poem is a lullaby,
my kin born of my kin. I am a space as much as I am a voice. Did you truly hail me
                    for a dim-witted conversation about love?
Me? There is nothing like me. I am no more like my siblings or my parents
                    than I am like a placid lake,
or the Gaping from which I was born. I am a charioteer, a bird.
                    Would you believe me if I said I also made
the Ether and the Day? Whether or not your faith is stored in my ear,
                    I am sure in what I have made.

How could I be both gentle enough and dangerous enough for your thoughts?
Do you have thoughts? I asked about moon,
dark, pain; you only gave me yourself. And as to my other question: it was me.
I invaded the day. It didn't stand a chance.

ARROW

((●

No one likes an essay that begins with a remark about the birth of Earth.
Still, indulge me. I know that the impulse to imagine a universal shift
is ungraceful, and the imagined universes born of that impulse are false ones, those in
which the imaginer alone lives. Still, I wonder about those classified as *diurnal*,
a category into which I reluctantly fit. I wonder if the vagaries of weather
hurt them more, whether they can feel each planetary movement, pulsing and round.

☾

Picture, for a moment, ire. Imagine everyone you know wishes you dead.
Imagine their wishes as a planet. Worlds such as this have terrible gravity:
fit to lasso moons, to make them crash to the ground in a blur.
Imagine your body composed of the dust they left behind. Every planet roils
with the gravity made by some ordinary evil. On worlds such as this, eclipses
don't come from the atmosphere. They are born of a curse.

«

Time, though I will hate you for it: stay slow.
Whet, on our imaginations, your tooth.
Raise from their infant forms your shadows.
Heed, and make sure they keep, their breath.
Time, if you must picture me, imagine me not too alone.
Time, if you must attend to me, please, wait.

(

This line marks a place from which Earth looks dead.
This line marks a place in which no memory ever blurs.
This line marks my childhood vision of incapacitation via eclipse.

(

Unlike many others, Archilochus wasn't afraid of the eclipse.
Or rather: for him, the *dread fear* the eclipse inspired always blurred
with *amazement*, and so what he actually feared was the death of fear, the gravity
of the consequences of its absence. What if *nothing amazes now*. What if the courses
of the stars might render everything ordinary, since now light has been pronounced dead
even as sun was shining. What if wonder, drained of blood, away from us could roll.

❝

By now you must be long in tooth,
skeletal and lacking in breath.
What fantasy of denouement makes you so willing to wait
for this story's end? Do you imagine you will find my fears defeated, me no longer alone
and abruptly willing to embrace both myself and my shadow,
no longer forcing you to think of degradation and loss, or of time as slow?

◖

If it is the last thing I do, I'll command you to be amazed. Seas rolling
onto the shore, dried to salt. The dust of growing gorges. The eclipse.
Fields of pines—no, full coasts—caught flame. Nebulae, dead,
their starred knots unknotted, dispersed and flayed into the dark. Blurs
of mackerel skies, horse-shaped clouds. The courses
set into motion by each loss of life. The persistence of gravity.

（

As a child of Icarus, I've a desire to chase the sun. And so lunar eclipses
have fallen from this accounting, which is in part a corrective, as the moon's blurred
light has long been more interesting to me than the sun's, living or dead.

((●

All diurnal animals are the children of Icarus, even during nocturnes. In
this we are unlucky, because the light we structure our lives around
lacks consolation. Baudelaire hated night because of the stars: why torment diurnal
things, who already lack respite from the glints of the earth.
The light already governs us even by its small changes, which cause space to shift.
None of this should be understood to mean that the night brings no cruel weather.

☽

I imagine there is an open secret among astronomers: charting a course
through either space or time will be impossible until both concepts have long been dead.
Sometimes, I imagine astronomers are also keeping secret the true cause of the solar eclipse.
Perhaps it comes when a critical mass of people at once try to imagine alternatives to gravity.
The eclipse, therefore, is a rebuttal. *I can steal your wonder. The orbits will never cease to roll.*
I can make you gather and stare as, perhaps once or twice in your small lives, night and day blur.

☽

Beyond the honeyed moon, Earth is a blur.
From this spot, my vision resembles what hounds see while coursing.
In today's main visio, this world looks like the tumbleweed's roll.
I know nothing about tumbleweed, except that they belong to the species *Kali,* the dead's
heroine and shepherd. A woman like that, she teaches you things about gravity.
A woman like that, to certain kinds of beloveds, is an eclipse.

"

Arrow, though I believe you to be a tool of devotion, I am drawn most to the shadow your figure impresses on my brutalities, like how the word for your home describes me when I wait, discomfited, unable to sit still, secretly running my tongue along my sharp and crooked tooth.

❝

Arrow, though this usage of you has fallen from favor, you are also a verb, as is tooth.
Neither verb has a reputation for patience, which is why I must wait,
likely for a long time, for them to come back into prominence within my shadows.

((●

Truth be told, I have never lacked for amazement, around
which I build even my pettiest visions, as reliably as the life of Earth
is built around both the sun and the moon, which dictate its weathers.
This also means I have also always held an affinity for fear, for shifting
uneasily toward the next dazzling thing. For the categories of *nocturnal* and *diurnal*
alike, not to mention *crepuscular* and *cathemeral*, the uncanny is the house best lived in.

☾

You need to know that the moment I say something's *persistent*, as I have here with gravity,
I immediately imagine it vanished. I'm not so selfish to believe my imagination, roil
as it may within me, is by any means an accurate depiction of planetary courses.
Barthes called "I" the pronoun of the imaginary: what is an "I" to an eclipse?
Still, I do imagine, and wantonly, uninterested in fidelity, even at its most blurred.
Hear me: faith is no way to learn that you are not dead.

❝

What am I to the aftereffects of murder, to the robbed breath.
What am I to the blind faith in an interlocutor sustained by each person alone.
What am I to eons of time, water over and over, to the mountains built slowly,
to the colors in which my dead appear to me, like shadow-
blue, to the visios that grow with each flinch of the mind, lying in wait
for their moment, to the birds, those children of Icarus, who need neither devotion nor teeth.

❨❨●

Because nothing but looking seems like life to me, I am often overcome by the weather, prone to singing praises and dirges and prone to allegories of paradise and of hell. In this I believe you and I are the same. Let us hold each other to this apocalyptic earth.

❝

It's not kind of me to say, but I don't always love you, sitting there waiting
for me to finish, humming along with a throaty voice that moves slow
and low. Or maybe you're moving these pages frenetically in the dark, fast and alone,
like you do with porn, your phone's glint reflected in your teeth,
which are bared because you are taking pains to ensure that your increasingly heavy breath
alerts no one to even the hint of a libido you might have, stirs not a single shadow.

❨❨●

Some of my favorite words mean wildly contrary things. Such is true of *shift*,
which means, among other things, *beginning* and *last resort*. Or *marigolds*—more diurnal
children—which means both *worries* and those round-
eyed, red-golden flowers. O, my spirit, stay with me through this weather.
It is true that you are dear to me and true also that my love has changed you, and yours, in
me, has grown roots, which fasten me to this violently bucking earth.

"

It's no kinder of me to say how much I do love you, how I won't move an inch until your shadow,
in its entirety, has disappeared beyond the moons of Saturn, how, each time it has, I wait
with my own increasingly heavy breath
for your return, which is always slower
than I want it to be, how sometimes my visio in your absence is of my own teeth
lit on fire by the oxygen gasped out of me, how, without you, I am, comprehensively, alone.

❲❲●

Stasis is as uninteresting as *progress*, much like the question of whether
to be *optimistic* or *pessimistic*, especially as we arrow from times of grief into—
well, into more such times. A secret: although I have yearned, sometimes acutely, to shift
my spirit into harder-toothed customs, even when bereft it's none other than *love* around
which all of my thoughts cluster like prehistoric moths learning the glints of the earth
in an ancient epoch as unkind as this one, in which the rhythm of pain too was diurnal.

◖◖●

How then are we expected to bear our weight. We who are diurnal.
We, the subjects of—and, often, the causes of—the vagaries of the weather.
We subjects. I understand why you might assume I believe in a divine; no earthly
or heavenly house is unchanged by my imagination, and my mouth is always frozen in
an O, which means both lack and plenty, which is astonishment made round
as a pair of lips from which a tongue is missing. My love is my utter, final shift.

❝

You, O spirit, are my one organ alone.
You are searching for ways to acquiesce to your shadow.
You are priming yourself to be capable of using your sharpest tooth.
You tell yourself, as I do, to learn how to wait.
And, conversely, how to stop waiting, when to do so would be detrimentally slow.
You must learn how to stop counting your breaths.

◖◖●

O, world, you have me, and I do love you, and I do feel devotion toward you, *Earth,*
all the light-bearing spheres, rhymes, constellations, flowers, the dead, all that dwell inside
this terrifying *home* of a word, this word that quickens the blood, weathered.

O

Stars are not the end, but the
beginning.

A bird is to its throat as a promise is
to its sharp edge.

I wanted to make for you a
sun-shower. Instead I have made for
you a mortal thing.

Writing is knowing how to cut.

There is a space in my body that did
not exist when I began this book. It
is a window. When I next speak, I
will do so through that window.

Please leave the window unlatched.

When I next speak, it will be with
changed lips.

I wonder what their color will be.

*Finally, she enlarges the figure to a grand
scale, and cuts off its head.*

NOTES

*In an attempt to curb my instinct toward the citationally Borgesian, I have limited these
notes to direct, intentional provenances that the poems themselves do not fully explain.
Other voices and referents, thankfully and invariably, also lurk. One example of a lurker
I will permit myself to share with you, because I recently reacquainted myself with it and
I hope that you might read or reread it: Carl Phillips's "As from a Quiver of Arrows" has
long haunted my mind. There are no explicit references to it in this book, and I don't think
I reread it while writing this book. But I recently returned to it and reread it, and so it felt
strange not to mention it and my gratitude for it here.*

"Marigolds" contains and adapts lines from and references to Robert Lowell, *Titus
Andronicus*, Deborah Digges, the *Homeric Hymns*, James Merrill, and Lucille Clifton, as
well as a few newspaper headlines. It also contains and adapts lines from the chorus of
"Down to the River" by The Brothers Comatose. The title comes by way of the French word
soucis, which means both "worries" and "marigolds."

The title of "Most of the Children Who Lived in This House Are Dead. As a Child I
Lived Here. Therefore I Am Dead" is inspired by one example of what Michel Foucault calls
an "enthymeme" in *History of Madness*, and its phrase "A child is being beaten" comes from
Sigmund Freud.

In "Dear, beloved" are lines that are adaptations of or contain references to Albert

Millican's *Travels and Adventures of an Orchid Hunter*, Hesiod, Tom Waits's "Dirt in the Ground," *Beowulf*, Nina Simone, *Bloom* by Anna Schuleit Haber, Italo Calvino, and other sources mentioned either more obliquely or directly. Its title comes from the English-language translation of the Sanskrit-origin name *Priya*.

The first line of "O Spirit [A bear brings forth her young]" comes from Sir Thomas Browne's *Vulgar Errors*.

"O Spirit [I wish to lay before you]" is comprised of phrases from *Moby-Dick*.

The italicized questions in "Basic Questions" come from Lucille Clifton's spirit writing. Due to a typographical disruption, it's hard to tell whether the word I have rendered here as "earth" is indeed "earth" or in fact "death." (My gratitude to Lynn Keller for this observation.)

The lines of poetry to which I refer in "Essay on Devotion" are from Lucie Brock-Broido's "Still Life with Aspirin" (in which she is referring to lines from Wallace Stevens); the italicized lines in the first sentence of the fourth verse paragraph are from Foucault's *History of Madness*.

"Windows" began as a series of my own translations of Rainer Maria Rilke's "Les Fenêtres" lyric sequence. Over a period of years, I then altered their syntax, line breaks, stanza breaks, and words; extracted individual phrases via erasure; and created from those phrases fifty-two short sections.

Two lines in "Arrow [Was it I who invaded the day]" come from or are direct references to the words of Louise Bourgeois, including one entry in her series *What Is the Shape of This Problem?* and including her contribution to the Tate Modern's Unilever Series; the phrases "X is an obstruction" and "the poetry of X was music" are from Wallace Stevens's "The Creations of Sound."

The first italicized line in "O" is from Georges Didi-Huberman. The second comes from an image caption in the 2017-2018 exhibit of Bourgeois's work at the Museum of Modern Art in New York.

RECENT TITLES FROM ALICE JAMES BOOKS

Country, Living, Ira Sadoff
Hot with the Bad Things, Lucia LoTempio
Witch, Philip Matthews
Neck of the Woods, Amy Woolard
Little Envelope of Earth Conditions, Cori A. Winrock
Aviva-No, Shimon Adaf, Translated by Yael Segalovitz
Half/Life: New & Selected Poems, Jeffrey Thomson
Odes to Lithium, Shira Erlichman
Here All Night, Jill McDonough
To the Wren: Collected & New Poems, Jane Mead
Angel Bones, Ilyse Kusnetz
Monsters I Have Been, Kenji C. Liu
Soft Science, Franny Choi
Bicycle in a Ransacked City: An Elegy, Andrés Cerpa
Anaphora, Kevin Goodan
Ghost, like a Place, Iain Haley Pollock
Isako Isako, Mia Ayumi Malhotra
Of Marriage, Nicole Cooley
The English Boat, Donald Revell
We, the Almighty Fires, Anna Rose Welch
DiVida, Monica A. Hand
pray me stay eager, Ellen Doré Watson
Some Say the Lark, Jennifer Chang
Calling a Wolf a Wolf, Kaveh Akbar
We're On: A June Jordan Reader, Edited by Christoph Keller and Jan Heller Levi
Daylily Called It a Dangerous Moment, Alessandra Lynch
Surgical Wing, Kristin Robertson
The Blessing of Dark Water, Elizabeth Lyons
Reaper, Jill McDonough
Madwoman, Shara McCallum
Contradictions in the Design, Matthew Olzmann
House of Water, Matthew Nienow
World of Made and Unmade, Jane Mead

Alice James Books is committed to publishing books that matter. The press was founded in 1973 in Boston, Massachusetts as a cooperative, wherein authors performed the day-to-day undertakings of the press. This element remains present today, as authors who publish with the press are invited to collaborate closely in the publication process of their work. AJB remains committed to its founders' original feminist mission, while expanding upon the scope to include all voices and poets who might otherwise go unheard. In keeping with its efforts to build equity and increase inclusivity in publishing and the literary arts, AJB seeks out poets whose writing possesses the range, depth, and ability to cultivate empathy in our world and to dynamically push against silence. The press was named for Alice James, sister to William and Henry, whose extraordinary gift for writing went unrecognized during her lifetime.

Designed by Tiani Kennedy
Printed by McNaughton & Gunn